EPHESIANS

BRINGING THE BIBLE TO LIFE

Genesis, by John H. Walton, Janet Nygren, and Karen H. Jobes
  (12 sessions)

Esther, by Karen H. Jobes and Janet Nygren
  (8 sessions)

John, by Gary M. Burge, Karen Lee-Thorp, and Karen H. Jobes
  (12 sessions)

Romans, by Douglas J. Moo, Karen Lee-Thorp, and Karen H. Jobes
  (12 sessions)

Ephesians, by Klyne Snodgrass, Karen Lee-Thorp, and Karen H. Jobes
  (6 sessions)

Hebrews, by George H. Guthrie, Janet Nygren, and Karen H. Jobes
  (8 sessions)

BRINGING
THE
BIBLE
TO LIFE

EPHESIANS

Living the Faith

Klyne Snodgrass
Karen Lee-Thorp
Series Editor, Karen H. Jobes

ZONDERVAN.com/
AUTHORTRACKER
follow your favorite authors

ZONDERVAN°

Bringing the Bible to Life: Ephesians
Copyright © 2008 by Klyne Snodgrass, Karen Lee-Thorp, and Karen H. Jobes

ISBN 978-0-310-27654-8

Interior design by Michelle Espinoza

Printed in the United States of America

CONTENTS

SERIES PREFACE

Have you ever been in a small-group Bible study where the leader read a passage from the Bible and then invited the members of the group to share what the passage meant to them? God wants to speak to each person individually through the Bible, but such an approach to group study can often be a frustrating and shallow experience for both leader and participants. And while the same passage can speak in various ways into people's lives, the meat of the Word is found in what the biblical writer intended to say about God and our relationship to him. The Bringing the Bible to Life series is for those who are ready to move from a surface reading of the Bible into a deeper understanding of God's Word.

But the Bible, though perhaps familiar, was written in ancient languages and in times quite different from our own, so most readers need a bit more help getting to a deeper understanding of its message. A study that begins and ends with what a passage "means to me" leaves the meaning of the passage unanchored and adrift in the thoughts—and perhaps the misunderstanding—of the reader. But who has time to delve into the history, language, cultures, and theology of the Bible? That's the work of biblical scholars who spend their lives researching, teaching, and writing about the ancient Scriptures. The need is to get the fruit of all that research into the hands of those in small-group Bible studies.

Zondervan's NIV Application Commentary (NIVAC) series was written to bring the best of evangelical biblical scholarship to those who want to know *both* the historical meaning of the biblical text *and* its contemporary significance. This companion series, Bringing the Bible to Life, is intended to bring that material into small-group studies in an easy-to-use format. Pastors, Christian education teachers, and small-group leaders whether in church, campus, or home settings will find these guides to be an enriching resource.

Each guide in the series provides an introduction to the biblical book that concisely summarizes the background information needed to better understand the original historical context. Six to twelve sessions per guide, with each session consisting of eleven or twelve discussion questions, allow a focused study that moves beyond superficial Bible reading. Relevant excerpts from the corresponding NIVAC commentary provide easy access into additional material for those interested in going even deeper. A closing section in each session assists the group in responding to God's Word together or individually. Guidance for leading each session is included, making the task of small-group leadership more manageable for busy lives.

If you want to move from the biblical text to contemporary life on solid ground, this series has been written for you.

Karen H. Jobes, PhD
Gerald F. Hawthorne Professor of
New Testament Greek and Exegesis
Wheaton College and Graduate School

AUTHOR'S PREFACE

The letter of Ephesians remains as compelling to me as ever, and I remain convinced of this letter's power to change both the character of churches and the lives of individuals. I am eager for small groups to work through this study guide, for I am confident that it will assist people to grasp the thought of the letter more easily and also will create opportunities for understanding how the letter is to be lived out in daily life.

Based on my *NIV Application Commentary: Ephesians* (Zondervan, 1996), this study guide was prepared by Karen Lee-Thorp, and I am especially appreciative of her work. Also I want to thank Karen Jobes, who has overseen the whole process. May those who use the guide and commentary encounter the work of God's Spirit in their lives.

Klyne Snodgrass
Paul W. Brandel Professor of New Testament Studies
North Park Theological Seminary

INTRODUCTION

WHO ARE YOU?

Who are you? After we give our names, many of us have no idea how to answer this question. We might identify ourselves by the work we do or the roles we play: I'm a lawyer. I'm a teacher. I'm Dave's wife. I'm mom to three kids, and I work part-time at the bank.

Because everybody needs an identity, even if we don't use the word, some of us define ourselves by the bands or sports teams we like, the clothes we wear, the neighborhood we live in, or the ethnic group we come from. Religion is another identity marker, so we might add, "I'm a Christian."

But what does "I'm a Christian" mean? Does it mean we like to spend a couple of hours on a Sunday singing a certain kind of music and listening to a certain kind of motivational talk? Does it mean we like this radio station, that TV program, and these books? Is it a cultural label?

Ephesians is Paul's effort to help us figure out who we are. He's not just saying, "These are the beliefs about how to get into heaven that a Christian holds." He's saying, "This is who a Christian is. This is how he or she thinks and lives." Christ should affect everything about how we see ourselves and others. Paul speaks of being "in Christ" as if Christ were a country we're citizens of. He wants to grip us with just how different our home country is from the place where unbelievers live.

His goal isn't to make us feel pleased with ourselves that we're so much better than non-Christians. He's not trying to make us patriotic about our "team." Instead, he wants to rekindle the joy and hope that come when we get our minds around what God has done for us. He wants to motivate us to live in the radical, costly way that makes sense for a person "in Christ." And he wants us to experience the power of God to live as we otherwise couldn't.

PAUL

Paul was a Jew—well educated, thick skinned, and hardheaded—who came to believe that Jesus was the Jewish Messiah (Greek, "Christ"). He also came to believe that the benefits of allegiance to Christ were available not just to those who were born Jewish or who adopted Jewish culture, but for non-Jews (Gentiles) too. He spent decades of his life traveling through what is now Turkey, Greece, and the Balkans, telling people about Christ. He did prison time in various cities, after being charged that his teaching disturbed the peace. During one of these prison stays late in his life he wrote the letter called Ephesians.

EPHESUS?

Ephesus was a major port city on the coast of what is now Turkey. "Ephesians," the traditional name for this letter, suggests that Paul sent it to the Christians in Ephesus, just as he sent Romans to the Christians in Rome. In fact, Ephesians 1:1 says, "To God's holy people in Ephesus." But the TNIV has this footnote: "Some early manuscripts do not have *in Ephesus*." In fact, the earliest manuscript we have of this letter doesn't include those words. Also, Paul spent more than two years in Ephesus and "was emotionally attached to the believers there,"[1] yet Ephesians 1:15; 3:3–4; and 6:23–24 sound like comments from a writer who hasn't met his readers personally. So it's likely that Paul wrote Ephesians as a "circular letter" to be carried from town to town in the greater Ephesus area and read aloud to believers in each place. There are a number of towns near Ephesus where there were probably small gatherings of believers.

Whether Ephesians was first sent to Ephesus or not doesn't affect its status as God's Word. However, some scholars question whether Paul wrote it. Even though all of the manuscripts we have name Paul as author (1:1), these scholars argue that the language and theology of Ephesians differ enough from Paul's other letters to raise the question of whether he was in fact the author. Although it's fair to raise the question, the evidence against Paul's authorship is not compelling and the theory has its own set of problems. Even if Ephesians diverges 5 or 10 percent from the style of Paul's other letters, that divergence can be accounted for by the type of letter it is, its audience, and other such factors.[2]

Paul says he's writing from prison (3:1), so the date of the letter depends on which of his prison stays he's talking about. He could be writing in about AD 55 from a prison in Ephesus, in about AD 58 from Caesarea (on the coast of Palestine), or in about AD 60 from Rome. We lean toward Rome.

IDENTITY AND POWER

Normally we study a biblical book chapter by chapter. But in Ephesians Paul addresses a handful of themes over and over, and it's helpful to see how he deals with each of these throughout the letter. Therefore, we'll take each theme in turn. They aren't the only important issues the book raises, but these six themes are both essential and easily misunderstood:

Identity: Who are we? What does it mean to say we're "in Christ," as if Christ were a country we're citizens of?

Old/New Life: How is our life now, in Christ, radically different from the reality we'd be living in if we weren't joined to Christ?

Ethics: How does a Christian live?

Mutual Submission: Submission isn't a popular word these days. What does Paul mean by it? What does it look like to live from, in, to, and for the Lord?

Faith: What does faith have to do with our minds? And how is it more than just something that happens in our heads?

Power: Living like a Christian isn't easy. In fact it's impossible—without Christ. What power does God offer us, and how do we connect with it?

God loves us, has chosen us, and is blessing and transforming us. For Paul, even when he's sitting in prison, that's amazingly good news.

NOTES

1. Klyne Snodgrass, *NIV Application Commentary: Ephesians* (Grand Rapids, Mich.: Zondervan, 1996), 21.
2. See Snodgrass, 23–30, for further discussion.

WHO WE ARE IN CHRIST

Ephesians 1:1–14; 2:1–22

Cold winters with long nights, short days, and plenty of snow are facts of life in Minnesota. They are woven into Minnesotan identity along with traits and values inherited from Scandinavian forebears. Minnesotans value hardiness; they find ways to enjoy winter, such as snowmobiling, skating, or ice fishing; they know how to drive on snow and ice.

Southern Californians know how to drive on eight-lane freeways that branch into other eight-lane freeways. Sunshine, the beach, the desert, ethnic diversity—and earthquakes, drought, wildfires, and flash floods—shape their identity.

Where we live affects who we are in ways we may not even notice. After all, everybody around us is dealing with the same climate, terrain, and local values. Paul's readers all live in what is now Turkey, but he wants them to think of themselves as residents of an even more important geography: a place he calls "in Christ."

BLESSINGS IN CHRIST[1]

Read Ephesians 1:1–14.

1. Make a list of everything Paul says here that is true of us because we are "in Christ" (or "in him," etc.).

"In Christ" describes the oneness with Christ that determines who we truly are. Whether we live in California, Minnesota, Nigeria, or China, if we're Christians, then Christ himself is (or should be) the terrain, climate, history, and values that define us. That doesn't mean we'll all be the same (Chinese Christians are bound to be different from American Christians), but our deepest identity comes from Christ.

"[Christ] is the 'sphere of influence' or 'power field' in which [Christians] live and from which they benefit and are transformed. That is, his Spirit, values, character, history, and purposes shape their lives."[2] Christ is still a person, not a force field, but we need to learn to think of ourselves as living in him.

2. How does a person come to be "in Christ" (1:13)?

3. How is your identity influenced by the physical place where you live, or where you come from? (For example, how are you a Californian, a Southerner, a Chicagoan, an American, a Korean-American?)

GOING DEEPER

The Christian faith is not an attractive set of ideas or a nice avenue to follow. Rather, it is so deep an engagement with Christ, so deep a union with our Lord, that Paul can only describe it as living *in Christ*. To live in Christ is to be determined by him. He shapes who we are. A person cannot be conscious of being enveloped by Christ and behave in ways totally out of keeping with his character.[3]

We are saved *in* Christ and our thinking and behavior are transformed *in* Christ. As Paul says, Christians are becoming "holy and blameless" (1:4).

4. What difference does it make to your life that you live in two locales: a physical place and in Christ?

5. What does it mean "to be holy and blameless in his sight" (1:4)?

IN SIN OR IN CHRIST[4]

Read Ephesians 2:1 – 10.

6. Before we lived in Christ, we lived somewhere very different. What key elements of that environment influenced our identity then (2:1 – 3)?

"This world" (2:2) doesn't mean the natural world of rocks, plants, and animals. God created those, and they are good (Gen. 1:31). "This world" for Paul means the human world system (politics, economics, social customs) that ignores God.

"The ruler of the kingdom of the air" (2:2) is the devil. "The ancient world apparently viewed the air between heaven and earth as the domain of spirits."[5]

The phrase "sinful nature" (2:3) is in the original Greek the word "flesh." Paul doesn't mean that our physical bodies are bad. Rather, "flesh" for him means "that which is *merely human* and left to its own devices"[6] without God. God made us with human desires and instinctive drives, but apart from him those desires and drives take over like weeds and become distorted and compulsive "cravings."

7. When we changed realms from being "in sin" to "in Christ," we were included in some important things that had happened to Christ: his resurrection from the dead and his ascension into the heavenly realms (2:4–6). What do you think it means to say that "in Christ" we are seated right now with him in the heavenly realms?

GOING DEEPER

In Paul's mind, Christ's death and resurrection are not merely events that produce benefit for believers, they are events in which believers are included.... [P]eople either live in sin and under its influence or in Christ and under his influence. It is a question of serving the tyrant sin or the Lord Christ. Conversion is a transfer from one sphere to the other, a change of lordships, and being raised with Christ is the language Paul uses to describe this transfer from the realm of death to the realm of life.[7]

UNITED WITH GOD'S PEOPLE IN CHRIST[8]

Read Ephesians 2:11–22.

Being in Christ also means being connected to everyone else who is in him. Each of us is like one stone in a holy temple built "in the Lord" (note the repeated words "on," "in," and "by" in 2:20–22).

Today we tend to think of ourselves as individuals making our own free choices and determining our own destiny. But in the ancient East, people thought of themselves as connected, as a part of their families or tribes.

8. How easy is it for you to think of yourself as part of Christ, intimately connected to him and to others who are in him (2:19–22)? What helps or hinders you from thinking of yourself that way?

Because all Christians are in Christ, ethnic barriers like the one between Jews and Gentiles are (or should be) torn down between us. In Christ is "peace" (2:14, 17) between groups who were formerly hostile. In him groups that were "foreigners and strangers" (2:19) become family. Regardless of race, gender, or culture, "[w]e are one with all others in Christ whether we like it or not."[9]

9. How should being in Christ affect the way we relate to believers from different ethnic groups?

What about how we relate to believers who make a lot less money than we do?

10. If Paul is right, why do our churches tend to segregate people along ethnic and social lines?

11. What makes you feel that you belong, or don't belong, in the church?

Paul asks us to remember that we are alive "in Christ." "Remembering requires attention; it does not happen automatically. To apply this text means that time will be given to thinking, reading, discussing, and learning about the change God has brought. Remembering will lead to prayer and an awareness of God's presence and his involvement in what we do."[10] Because we automatically think of ourselves as individuals, defining our identity in worldly terms, we need to remind ourselves of who we are "in Christ."

12. What aspect of being "in Christ" is most significant for the way you see yourself currently?

RESPONDING TO GOD'S WORD

IN YOUR GROUP:

Ephesians 1:3–14 is in the form of a hymn of praise. Have someone read the following paraphrase aloud, and then let others respond with their own words of praise for what God has done for you in Christ.

How marvelous God is! His Spirit has provided everything needed for life. Every good thing has been made available in Christ. We praise such a God.

Right from the first God has been busy devising a way to draw us home to himself so that we may live with him and for him. Through Jesus Christ he has made us family. As a result we owe God praise for the way he freely gave himself to us in Christ. In Christ's death God's abundant care for us is known; God gave himself for us to bring us back and make us his people. What lavish love he has for us! We honor you, God.

In his unfathomable wisdom God has made known his plan and desire to bring all things together in Christ. This includes everything in our world and everything in God's world. Amazingly God's plan includes us and gives us a share in what he is doing. For this we owe God praise for the hope that is ours in Christ. When we heard about the truth from God and believed the good news about his plan, God marked us as his own by giving us his Spirit. The Spirit's dwelling in us is a pledge from God that he will complete his plan and that one day we will truly live with God. For this we owe God praise. Our God, we do worship you.[11]

ON YOUR OWN:

Choose something that is true of you because you are in Christ. (For example, you are one of God's chosen ones in Christ. Or you are forgiven in Christ. Or you belong as much as any other Christian belongs. You are no longer an outsider.) Write this truth at the top of a piece of paper, then write out how you respond to this thought. What do you feel when you think about this part of your identity? Does this truth conflict with something else about how you see yourself? (For instance, maybe you're used to seeing yourself as a loner or an exile.) If this truth is true, how should it or does it affect your life? What do you want to say to God in response?

NOTES

1. This section is based on *The NIV Application Commentary: Ephesians* (hereafter referred to as *NIVAC: Ephesians*) by Klyne Snodgrass (Grand Rapids, Mich: Zondervan, 1996), 37–69.
2. Snodgrass, 40.
3. Snodgrass, 42.
4. This section is based on *NIVAC: Ephesians*, 93–122.
5. Snodgrass, 97.
6. Snodgrass, 98.
7. Snodgrass, 102.
8. This section is based on *NIVAC: Ephesians*, 123–156.
9. Snodgrass, 150.
10. Snodgrass, 148.
11. Snodgrass, 69.

OLD LIFE, NEW LIFE

Ephesians 2:1–22; 4:17–24

The transformation of Ebenezer Scrooge is so compelling that Charles Dickens' *A Christmas Carol* has been staged and filmed in countless different productions. Readers and viewers come back to it Christmas after Christmas. We long to believe that truth and love can so grip Scrooge's imagination that they overcome more than six decades of his ingrained habits and revolutionize his life.

At some level, we know Scrooge's story is supposed to be our story. But when we look back on our lives, many of us feel deep down that we were never as bad as Scrooge. And when we look at our lives now, we have to admit that we're not bounding around with joy and generosity the way Scrooge does at the end of the story. Maybe, like Scrooge, we need a guide to take us on a tour of our past and present. Maybe we need a hard look at who we were (and would be now) apart from Christ. And maybe we need to stretch our vision of who we are (or could be now) in Christ. This is the guided tour Paul offers us.

DEAD OR ALIVE[1]

Read Ephesians 2:1–10.

Five times in Ephesians, Paul contrasts who we used to be with who we are now. This first time, in 2:1 – 10, he contrasts being dead in sin with being alive in Christ. For Paul, who believes "life comes from God and is experienced in relation to God,"[2] separation from God is a living death. The life separated from God is a constant quest for meaning.

1. Is existence without Christ as bad as Paul portrays it in 2:1 – 3? What evidence do you see for or against this view?

GOING DEEPER

Sin is the act of choosing our own way and leaving God out of the picture.... If God is the giver of life, every act that ignores God is sin. We have tried to find life in ourselves and our own desires, and in the process have cut ourselves off from the Giver of life and have crippled our relations with other people. Death—non-relational by definition—is the result.[3]

For Paul, even people who are largely good and decent have ultimately meaningless and sinful lives if they disregard God. They delude themselves into believing they define themselves and freely choose to do what they want, unaware that their wants are driven by self-seeking souls, a self-seeking society, and the Evil One.

2. Can a person agree with Paul about this world and still enjoy nature, the arts, and people—even unbelievers? Can such a person be involved in politics and society? Why or why not?

3. Paul thinks we should be extraordinarily grateful to be freed from living death. He thinks we should be even more grateful as we contemplate what we have in Christ. What significant features of life in Christ does he highlight in 2:4–10?

4. What could hinder a Christian from overflowing with gratitude and joy over this change of circumstances?

AT WAR OR AT PEACE[4]

Read Ephesians 2:11 – 22.

Paul's next sketch of life without Christ involves division, alienation, and lack of privileges (2:11 – 12). By contrast, life in Christ heals divisions, makes outcasts into family, and is rich in access to what matters (2:13 – 22).

5. If Christ had never come to earth, non-Jews would be "separate . . . excluded . . . foreigners . . . without hope . . . without God" (2:12). How easy or difficult is it for you to imagine this being the story of your life? Why is that?

The Jewish law was designed to separate Jews from Gentiles with its rules about food, circumcision, Sabbath, and other matters of daily life. Christ's death doesn't lessen the law as God's Word (it can still teach us a great deal about God and about life), but it does set aside the law "as a set of regulations that excludes Gentiles" from relationship with God or with Jews. "Jesus took the hostility of both Jews and Gentiles into himself, and when he died it died."[5]

6. Picture in your mind a wall with you on one side, and God and other people on the other side. As Christ dies, the wall crumbles. How easy is it for you to see yourself as a person without walls between you and God? Why is that?

How easy is it for you to see yourself as a person without walls between you and other Christians? Why is that?

Peace [2:14, 15, 17] is not merely the cessation of hostility; it is a comprehensive term for salvation and life with God. The background to this use is the Old Testament concept of *shalom*, which covers wholeness, physical well-being, prosperity, security, good relations, and integrity.[6]

7. The only command in all of Ephesians chapters 1 – 3 is "remember" (2:11). Why do you suppose Paul thinks it's so important for us to remember who we used to be and who we are now?

Why is it so easy for us to forget who we are in Christ?

Memories can be paths to success or scars that disable. Sometimes we choose to forget painful parts of life, but often only succeed in repressing the memory until a later, possibly more difficult, time. We also make choices in remembering as to how much attention will be given to particular painful or enjoyable events. Remembering is the way we name and process the past, the way we structure our minds to know how to live.[7]

OFF WITH THE OLD, ON WITH THE NEW[8]

Read Ephesians 4:17 – 24.

This dramatic change in who we are—alive, rescued, at peace, reconciled, included—should transform how we live. But how we live doesn't change automatically. We have to choose to stop thinking and living the way unbelievers do. Consider what Paul says about Christ-less thinking in 4:17 – 18. It is:

- Futile (meaningless, useless, empty), because it is ...
- Darkened (without guidance), because it is ...
- Separated from God's life-giving light, because people have ...
- Chosen not to know things they don't want to know, because they have ...
- Made their hearts hard, numb, insensitive.

8. Where do you see meaninglessness, lack of light and guidance, denial (refusal to know what's true), or insensitivity played out in our culture?

9. Paul says sensuality—preoccupation with sex, food, entertainment, and other material pleasures—takes over when an insensitive (numb) person gets desperate to feel something (4:19). How is that explanation different from the way people often justify sensual indulgence?

10. In contrast, we need to be made new in the attitude of our minds (4:23–24). How is Christ-centered thinking the opposite of what we've just described?

11. How does a Christ-centered person relate to physical pleasures (food, sex, entertainment, possessions)?

Sin is "a malfunction of the mind."[9] Conversion is the process of fixing our minds, and consequently our behavior. It may start with a one-time event, but "putting off" and "putting on" is the ongoing pattern by which we live. We renounce "a self-centered identity in favor of a Christ-defined identity. All that shapes us is given over to Christ, and his mindset of self-giving love becomes our mindset."[10] This happens through the Holy Spirit, as we cooperate with him and encounter God's love in the person of Christ.

12. How do you respond to the idea that conversion involves the Holy Spirit restructuring your thinking about everything, not just your beliefs about Jesus? What are the implications for your life?

RESPONDING TO GOD'S WORD

IN YOUR GROUP:

Have someone read aloud the following poem by seventeenth-century poet George Herbert.[11] Then respond with your own prayers of gratitude to God for delivering you from the old life of compulsive desires and futility, and giving you the new life you have now. These prayers can be as simple as one sentence: "Thank you, God, for _____."

LOVE (III)

Love bade me welcome, yet my soul drew back
    Guilty of dust and sin.
But quick-eyed Love, observing me grow slack
    From my first entrance in,
Drew nearer to me, sweetly questioning
    If I lacked anything.

"A guest," I answered, "worthy to be here";
    Love said, "You shall be he."
"I, the unkind, the ungrateful? ah my dear,
    I cannot look on thee."

Love took my hand and smiling did reply,
    "Who made the eyes but I?"

"Truth, Lord, but I have marred them; let my shame
    Go where it doth deserve."
"And know you not," says Love, "who bore the blame?"
    "My dear, then I will serve."
"You must sit down," says Love, "and taste my meat."
    So I did sit and eat.

ON YOUR OWN:

Reflect on George Herbert's poem above, and on what God has done for you. Write out a paragraph that describes specifically the old life from which God has delivered you. Write about your own experience of cravings, futility, denial, and insensitivity. Maybe you're all too aware of how those things are hanging on in your current life—if so, write down how they afflict you now. Then write a paragraph thanking God for delivering you from these things. Tell him how much it means to you that in Christ you can leave all that behind. Ask him for the grace to continually put off that old you and put on the new you that he created to be like him in true righteousness and holiness.

If moving your body helps you focus more than writing does, try taking a walk and talking to God about this.

NOTES

1. This section is based on *NIVAC: Ephesians*, 93–122.
2. Snodgrass, 95.
3. Snodgrass, 109.
4. This section is based on *NIVAC: Ephesians*, 123–156.
5. Snodgrass, 133.
6. Snodgrass, 130.
7. Snodgrass, 147.
8. This section is based on *NIVAC: Ephesians*, 228–246.
9. Snodgrass, 230.
10. Snodgrass, 240.
11. George Herbert, "Love (III)," *The Temple*, 1633 (some spelling modernized).

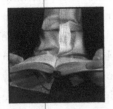

LIVING FAITH

Ephesians 2:8–10; 4:15, 25, 29; 5:8–14

Imagine a woman who goes through a wedding ceremony with her "true love." She pledges to have and to hold, from this day forward, in sickness and in health. But after the ceremony and reception, instead of moving in with her new husband, she goes back to her own apartment and continues to live like a single woman. She dates. She comes and goes as she pleases. But she wears her wedding ring and is happy to tell everyone she's married.

Most of us would agree that this isn't an innovative, grace-filled marriage. It's a non-marriage. This woman doesn't grasp that marriage is a covenant, a commitment to have a certain kind of day-after-day relationship. The vows aren't legalisms; they describe what marriage *is*.

Pledging faith in Christ is also a covenant, a commitment to a certain kind of day-after-day relationship. Paul compares faith to marriage explicitly in 5:23–32, but throughout Ephesians he presents faith as a relationship. Just as marriage is far more than saying, "I do," so faith is far more than saying, "I believe."

SAVED BY GRACE THROUGH FAITH[1]

Read Ephesians 2:8–10.

To be "saved" is to be rescued from the futile living death of our old lives. God has saved us by "grace"—"the completely undeserved, loving commitment of God to us. For some reason unknown to us, but which is rooted in his nature, God gives himself to us, attaches himself to us, and acts to rescue us. Though wrath should have come, saving grace comes instead. This action is rooted in God's very nature. The initiative always lies only and completely with him. No human action could remove us from the plight in which we are found."[2]

Grace connects us to Christ. Our faith doesn't save us; it's only the means by which we accept the gift.

> *For it is by grace you have been saved, through faith—and this is not from yourselves, it is the gift of God (Eph. 2:8).*

1. Why is it crucial for Christians to know that we're saved by grace?

GOING DEEPER

Faith (*pistis*) cannot be limited to mental assent or to believing certain ideas. The Greek noun can mean "faith," "faithfulness," "reliability," "promise," "pledge," "proof," "trust," and "confidence." ... The verb *pisteuo* can mean "trust," "give credence to," "be convinced that," "entrust," and "have confidence." Primarily, this word group treats *that on which one may rely* or *the act of relying on something believed reliable.*"[3]

2. How is relying on someone different from mentally accepting certain ideas?

Faith is relational, describing reliance on a reliable God. Faith is a *covenant* word, expressing the commitment and trust that bind two parties together.[4]

3. What has God done to deserve our reliance on him? What has he done to deserve our being faithful to him?

Faith is like glue. It binds us to the one we believe in. We are "in him," and what is true of him is true of us. He died; we died with him. He was raised to new life; we were raised with him. He reigns; we reign with him. "Salvation does not come from believing ideas or an emotional decision, but from being bound to Christ."[5]

4. It's impossible to be saved by "works" (2:9), our own accomplishments. But Paul says we are saved *for* works (2:10). What's the difference between being saved by works and being saved for works (2:9 – 10)?

Paul thinks faith changes lives and produces acts of love and Christlikeness. But many Christians today think it's only desirable, not necessary, that faith should lead to action. Some may think of faith as "[a] decision, the right prayer prayed, [which] is enough to go to heaven. How did faith in Christ get perverted into thought about Christ? How did all the focus get placed on getting into heaven? How did anyone read the New Testament and conclude we do not have to do anything?"[6]

5. How would you answer that question: "How did anyone read the New Testament and conclude we do not have to do anything?"

6. Does Paul mean that we "saved people" need to be constantly working, working, working to make God happy? Explain your view.

LIVE AS CHILDREN OF LIGHT[7]

Read Ephesians 5:8–14.

Paul has a lot to say about the kind of works that faith—our covenant relationship—will produce. One word picture he uses is light. The apostle John also speaks of light. God is light (1 John 1:5). Christ is the light of the world (John 8:12). If we are "in Christ"—living in him, joined in covenant to him—then we become light too.

7. What life habits does a child of light have (5:8–14)?

8. Why is light a fitting word picture to describe a person who lives his or her faith in the world?

DOING THE TRUTH IN LOVE[8]

Read Ephesians 4:15, 25, 29.

Faith/faithfulness is also linked to truth/truthfulness. We need to believe what is true (about Christ, about ourselves, about the world). We also need to *say* and *do* what is true.

"The word for 'truth' [in 4:15] is actually a verb; a literal translation is 'truthing in love.'"[9] In the Old Testament, truth is something God's people do as well as something we can rely on. It's a term of covenant relationship and loyalty. It's sometimes translated as "faithfulness."

GOING DEEPER

A truthful person is one who lives out his or her covenant obligations, which includes both what is said and what is done. Therefore, *both* truth and love bind us to the other person.... Truth involves a true assessment of the facts and a consideration of what is real as opposed to illusion, but it is much more holistic than what is done with the mind. [It joins what we say with what we do in our relationships with God and others.][10]

9. Why is love impossible without truthfulness/honesty/faithfulness?

10. If we tell each other the "truth" harshly or arrogantly, are we saying what is really true in God's eyes? Explain.

GOING DEEPER

[T]he gospel expresses reality, so speaking the truth in love involves rejecting the pseudo-reality in which our society seeks to live and embracing what is really real—God and his work in the world....

Living the truth in love is no abstract exercise; it is personal, practical, and all-embracing. No other foundation exists for healthy living. We as humans prefer to live in delusion, hiding from ourselves and thinking we are better (or worse) than we are. We lie to ourselves, to each other, and to God.[11]

11. Why are Christians often afraid to tell each other the truth about their sin or their pain?

How does deceiving each other in this way harm both us and our Christian communities?

GOING DEEPER

The thought that we can believe in Christ without being like him is absurd. If Christ's indwelling does not transform, we must question strenuously whether Christ is present. The application of the text of Ephesians requires us to test the validity of our faith (see 2 Cor. 13:5). Christians worry about the assurance of their salvation, and other Christians seek to remove all doubt. Maybe we should let doubt do its work. Maybe we should be more concerned about the validity of faith than the assurance of salvation. Honest doubt can be healthy.[12]

12. What do you think of the idea that honest doubt about the validity of our faith can be healthy? How might it be healthy or not healthy? What are the risks or benefits of honestly doubting our faith?

> *From the cowardice that shrinks from new truths,*
> *From the laziness that is content with half-truths,*
> *And from the arrogance that thinks it knows all truth,*
> *O God of truth, deliver us.*[13]

RESPONDING TO GOD'S WORD

IN YOUR GROUP:

"Worship is telling the truth about God. Confession is telling the truth about ourselves."[14] Spend some time telling the truth about God. Sing a song about who God is and what he has done in Christ. Or pray along these lines:

> *Lord, your love overflows so much that you chose us before we were made, adopted us to be your family, and rescued us from the futility of living death. Everything you've done for us is wholly undeserved. You are utterly reliable and faithful to your promises. You ask us to be faithful in return. You chose us not to remain in our self-centeredness, but to free us from our self-centeredness. Give us the grace to speak and do what is true. In Jesus' name, amen.*

After a time of worship, consider giving group members some time to say something that is true about themselves. Some sins are more appropriately confided to one or two mature people, but your group should be a place where people can tell more of the truth about themselves than they can safely tell casual acquaintances. A commitment to repeating nothing outside the group that is said in the group is essential. This is a basic rule of group faithfulness. Pray for those who share something they're struggling with.

ON YOUR OWN:

Write out a prayer in which you tell the truth about God and the truth about yourself. The prayer in 3:16–21, which you'll discuss in session 6, may be good to pray now. Pray for the grace to grasp how wide and deep is God's love for you, so that you are able to face and deal with the harder truths about yourself. Pray for Christ to dwell in your heart through true faith.

NOTES

1. This section is based on *NIVAC: Ephesians*, 104–107, 114, 120–122.
2. Snodgrass, 103.
3. Snodgrass, 104–105.
4. Snodgrass, 105.
5. Ibid.
6. Snodgrass, 114.
7. This section is based on *NIVAC: Ephesians*, 266–284.
8. This section is based on *NIVAC: Ephesians*, 215–217, 225–227, 249, 255–256, 261.
9. Snodgrass, 206.
10. Ibid.
11. Snodgrass, 225.
12. Snodgrass, 189.
13. Snodgrass, 227, quoting Henlee H. Barnette, "The Minister as a Moral Role-Model."
14. Snodgrass, 225.

RESPONDING TO GRACE

Ephesians 4:1–16; 4:25–5:2

A heavy drinker is partying with some friends on a yacht. He's so drunk that he falls overboard. The water is frigid, and he's too drunk even to reach and hang onto a life buoy tossed down to him. Just before he drowns, the only sober guest on the yacht jumps into the water and lashes him to the buoy so he can be hauled back on board. That guest suffers severely from the cold until the buoy can be tossed to him in turn. But eventually the rescuer returns to safety. Later that evening, however, having changed into dry clothes, the rescuer is astonished to see the man who nearly drowned drinking again, swearing at someone who suggests he's had enough, and roaming the deck unsteadily. The closest he gets to thanking his rescuer is saluting him with a half-emptied glass.

Most of us would agree that this man is at best ungrateful and at worst crazy. Neither his brush with death nor his costly rescue has moved him to change his behavior. He's like a Christian who thinks grace means being rescued from eternal torment and getting to live to please himself. Such a so-called Christian has failed to come to grips with what grace and salvation are about. In this session we'll continue to look at how we respond to what God has done for us in Christ.

A LIFE WORTHY OF YOUR CALL[1]

Read Ephesians 4:1 – 16.

1. Ephesians 4:1 summarizes Paul's ethical teaching: "live a life worthy of the calling you have received." How has Paul described your calling in 1:1 – 14 and 2:1 – 22?

2. Why do you think Paul wants awareness of what God has done for us in Christ to motivate our ethical behavior? Why isn't he content simply to tell us what the rules are?

GOING DEEPER

If God's love is so great, if his salvation is so powerful, if God has granted such reconciliation, then believers should live accordingly. They should value God's love enough to be shaped by it.... Obedience is always a response to grace. God acts first [creating us, saving us from sin and death, and giving us his Spirit], and humans respond.[2]

3. Humility (4:2) is the opposite of ego and self-centeredness. Why is self-centeredness unworthy of the calling we've received?

Gentleness (4:2) is the opposite of harshness, careless treatment of others, and violence. Why are these unworthy of our calling to be in Christ?

Patience (4:2) is willingness to set aside one's own agenda, giving others time and space to fail and learn. Why is that worthy of those who follow Christ?

In 4:1, 17; 5:2, 8, 15 Paul uses the verb "walk" (TNIV, "live") to describe the way we respond to what God has done. Walking is "controlled, enduring, and directed, not ... frenetic or aimless."[3] We consistently walk or live a certain way by our own choice and by the power of God's Spirit. We are neither passive nor helpless. "None of this suggests we accomplish anything by ourselves, but life with God and by his help is a life of discipline and effort. We want discipleship without discipline; it does not exist."[4]

4. What's your reaction to the idea that following Christ involves discipline and effort? Does that sound appealing or unappealing? Is it consistent with grace or opposed to grace? Explain.

Central to our calling as Christians is that we are called to be connected with each other "in Christ." Paul uses the metaphor of a human body (4:12, 16) to describe our interconnectedness. Just as diverse bones and muscles have different functions but are inseparably bound to work together, so Christians with diverse abilities are inseparably connected. We're completely unable to fulfill our purposes without working together. We are Christ's body here on earth, so unity (not uniformity) is essential.

5. How does Paul describe what unity is supposed to look like in 4:2 – 16?

GOING DEEPER

Most of the vices in the New Testament ethical instruction are sins that disrupt community, and most of the virtues promote community.

The ego is the main problem in relations, for therein lies the origin of feelings of inferiority and arrogance, of envy and greed, of prejudice and defensiveness, and of intolerance and abuse. As William Temple noted, pride is always the root of spiritual failure. The solution is in a sense of God's grace, for grace prevents the ego from inflating its own significance.[5]

FOLLOW GOD'S EXAMPLE[6]

Read Ephesians 4:25–5:2.

Qualities like humility, patience, and gentleness are appropriate responses to what Christ has done, partly because they reflect Christ's own character. He is the model of humility, patience, and gentleness rooted not in passive weakness but in strong character. Like Ephesians 4:1, Ephesians 5:1 also offers a summary of Paul's ethical teaching: "Follow God's example." We are able to do something as seemingly impossible as imitating God's character because he has adopted us as his dearly loved children and given us his Spirit. The Holy Spirit longs to work through us and is grieved (4:30) when we don't cooperate.

6. What motivations does Paul give for each of these instructions?

- Put off falsehood and speak truthfully (4:25), because . . .

- In your anger do not sin (4:26), because . . .

- Work instead of stealing (4:28), because . . .

- Don't say things that tear people down (4:29), because . . .

- Be kind and forgiving instead of bitter, quarreling, or malicious (4:31 – 32), because ...

- Walk in the way of love (5:2), because ...

7. Which of those motivations have to do with responding to what God has done for us?

Which of them have to do with reflecting God's character in our own actions?

8. Love is the sphere in which Christians are to live and walk (5:2). In 3:17 – 18, Paul prays that his readers will comprehend just how much God loves them. Deeply knowing we're loved is essential if we are to love others. What helps you know you're loved? Or what hinders you from fully believing it?

9. Paul keeps going back to the idea that we do what we do because we are Christ's body (4:4, 12 – 13, 15 – 16, 25). How easy is it for you to think of yourself as so connected to other Christians that you suffer or thrive, succeed or fail, grow to maturity or not, with them? What helps or hinders you in seeing your life this way?

Along with deceit, anger is one of the main killers of relationships within Christ's body. Anger against evil is justified, but human anger is usually destructive because it's usually self-centered. Anger communicates "what we care about — usually ourselves — and is an attempt at punishment. It is a chemical and physiological reaction to our displeasure that the world is not as we wish. It is also a choice we make, for we choose both what we react to and at what level the reaction will occur.... We express anger only where it is safe, and virtually never to those we fear or respect highly."[7]

10. If a person has trouble getting over anger (and thus goes to bed still mad, 4:26), struggles with bitterness, tends to get into arguments, or makes hostile jokes or comments (4:29–31), how can he or she overcome those habits?

11. How do you think other Christians should deal with a person like this? What would Paul say?

12. Does all this ethical teaching sound to you like legalistic rule-making cloaked in theological language? Why, or why not?

RESPONDING TO GOD'S WORD

IN YOUR GROUP:

As you'll discuss in session 6, the power to reflect Christ's character in your actions comes from God's Spirit working within you. You'll be gracious in response to God's grace, loving in response to God's love. Pray for a deeper awareness of his love for you. You might pray aloud Ephesians 3:16–21 or this prayer by the Armenian spiritual writer Gregory of Narek (AD 951–1003):[8]

> *Before I was, you created me.*
> *Before I could wish, you shaped me.*
> *Before I glimpsed the world's light, you saw me.*
> *Before I emerged, you took pity on me.*
> *Before I called, you heard me.*
> *Before I raised a hand, you looked over me.*
> *Before I asked, you dispensed mercy on me.*
> *Before I uttered a sound, you turned your ear to me.*
> *Before I sighed, you attended me.*
> *Knowing in advance my current trials,*
> *You did not thrust me from your sight.*
> *No, even foreseeing my misdeeds,*
> *you fashioned me.*
>
> *And now, do not let me*
> *whom you made, saved and took into*
> *your care, be lost to sin and*
> *the Troublemaker's deceptions.*
> *Do not let the fog of my willfulness prevail*
> *over the light of your forgiveness,*
> *nor the hardness of my heart*
> *over your long-suffering goodness,*
> *nor my mortal flaws*
> *over your perfect wholeness,*
> *nor my weak flesh*
> *over your invincible strength.*

ON YOUR OWN:

Choose one of the character traits discussed in this session that you would like to cultivate. Go for a walk and think about how God has treated you or someone else that way. If you need more patience, how has God been patient with you? If you feel bitter toward someone, how has God forgiven you? If you feel someone has hurt you far more than you have hurt God, reflect on Christ forgiving those who betrayed and killed him. If you find it hard to love someone, how is God loving you right now? Ask him to make you more deeply aware of his love for you.

NOTES

1. This section is based on *NIVAC: Ephesians*, 194–227.
2. Snodgrass, 196, 194.
3. Snodgrass, 217.
4. Ibid.
5. Snodgrass, 209.
6. This section is based on *NIVAC: Ephesians*, 247–265.
7. Snodgrass, 257.
8. St. Grigor Narekatsi, *Speaking with God from the Depths of the Heart: The Armenian Prayer Book of St. Gregory of Narek*, prayer 18, translated by Thomas J. Samuelian (Yerevan, Armenia: Vem Press, 2001). Used by permission of the translator.

IN, TO, AND FOR THE LORD

Ephesians 4:1–16; 5:15–6:9

I f our society has learned anything from history, it has learned to mistrust authority. Authority figures, we well know, often abuse their power. Husbands abuse wives. Parents abuse children. Management exploits workers. Political leaders use power for personal gain. Teachers, lawyers, doctors, clergy, CEOs—we've all heard of the scandals.

The only solution our society knows is to pass laws that spell out each person's rights. Then people can battle to ensure their rights aren't violated. Maybe that's the best a pluralist society can do, but Paul envisions a different pattern of relations between those who are "in Christ." For citizens of the heavenly realms, Christ is King, Master, Lord. We who mistrust authority flinch at the thought of trusting a king to command us. But Paul thinks that if we can get our minds around first submitting to Christ as Lord, then many other relationships fall into place.

LIVING FOR THE LORD[1]

In Ephesians 4:1 (compare 3:1) Paul calls himself a prisoner "for the Lord." Even in the most difficult of times his core identity is defined by his relationship with the Lord. All his teaching about human relationships flows from this idea of being "in" the Lord and of doing things for the Lord and as if they were done to the Lord. "Lord" is what Romans called Caesar, what Jews called God, what slaves called their masters.

1. Paul says we Christians have "one Lord" and "one God and Father of all, who is *over* all and through all and in all" (4:5–6, italics added). He says Christ is the head of the body we belong to, and that everything is *under* his feet (1:22–23; 4:15–16). How do you respond to this kind of hierarchical language? To what extent do you embrace it, and to what extent does it seem foreign or uncomfortable?

SUBMIT TO ONE ANOTHER[2]

Read Ephesians 5:15–5:21.

"The most difficult part of this text for ancient and modern readers is the expectation that Christians will submit to each other (5:21). Some have argued that mutual submission is illogical, which it *is*, if viewed apart from Christ."[3] The word translated "submit" means "to arrange under, to submit." That implies a hierarchy. But while everybody is below Christ (1:22), Paul says in 5:21 that all Christians should make a habit of putting themselves below all other Christians. "[T]his text does not ask some Christians to submit to other Christians. It asks *all* Christians to submit to *each other*. No privileged group is in view."[4]

Paul wants Christians to "reject self-centeredness and work for the good of others. Submission is nothing more than a decision about the relative worth of others."[5]

2. What attitudes toward other Christians will we have if we are submitting to one another out of reverence for Christ (5:21)?

3. What are some things we might do—or do differently—if we are submitting to each other?

GOING DEEPER

Our society emphasizes equality, but mutual submission is a much stronger idea. With equality, you still have a battle of rights. Equality can exist without love, but it will not create a Christian community. With mutual submission, we give up rights and support each other. Mutual submission is love in action. It brings equal valuing and is the power by which a *Christian* community establishes itself.[6]

4. What if we subordinate our own interests to another Christian's interests, but that person isn't interested in mutual submission? What if that person takes advantage of our commitment to mutual submission? How should we respond?

To add the idea of the "reverence of Christ" to submission only compounds our discomfort. "Reverence" (lit., "fear") expresses a recognition of the holiness of God and an awareness of being bound to him by his love.... Self-centeredness is jettisoned because one knows Christ is both loving Savior and coming Judge. Christ is a friend, but not just a friend. He is also Lord of the universe.[7]

GOING DEEPER

5. How will reverence for Christ affect the way we treat other people?

SUBMISSION IN THE HOUSEHOLD[8]

Read Ephesians 5:21–6:9.

Because the family household was (and is) the most basic unit in society, Paul wants Christians to live "in the Lord" in their family relationships. Roman households typically included at least one slave. In that hierarchical culture, everybody assumed that wives would obey their husbands, children would obey their fathers, and slaves, their masters. The attitude toward and standing of women was different within Judaism than in Roman society, but in both cultures women were expected to submit obediently to their fathers until marriage and then to their husbands. They were also expected to follow their father's or husband's religion. Slaves, whether male or female, were considered property. There was a range of views of how they should be treated, but violence toward them was commonplace.

Paul shocked his society by valuing women and slaves at the level of men and masters (Gal. 3:28). He told women they should be loyal to Christ even if their husbands opposed their faith (1 Cor. 7:15). And while his readers might have been reassured by his instructions to wives, children, and slaves in Ephesians 5:21–6:9 (since he wasn't completely undermining the social order), they would also have been astonished that Paul directly addressed wives and slaves, and astounded by his instructions to husbands. Instead of simply exhorting the weaker parties to submission and leaving it at that, he exhorted the party with the most power, the man, to mutual submission as well.

6. Imagine a man in Paul's day who has been brought up to believe women are inferior, less intelligent, and more prone to immorality than men. What in 5:25–32 do you think would surprise him and why?

7. Paul instructs husbands not only to love their wives, but to love them as Christ loved the church and gave himself up for her. What would it look like today for a man to deny his own self-interests for the good of his wife? Try to think of specific kinds of examples.

Headship (5:23) implies authority, but in this passage authority is redefined to focus on the responsibility of the husband to care for and nurture his wife. "Both partners live first of all in, to, and for the Lord. The real head of the marriage is *always* Christ, and both partners are to live in mutual submission to each other, seek to promote each other within the purposes of Christ, and live out the oneness of their relationship."[9]

8. Paul tells wives to submit to their husbands as part of their submission "to the Lord" (5:22). He tells children to submit to parents "in the Lord" (6:1). He tells slaves to obey and serve their masters as if they "were serving the Lord" (6:5–8). How should "to, in, and for the Lord" affect the way a person deals with every other person, whether that person is thought to be "under" one or in authority over one?

[Jesus said] "You know that the rulers of the Gentiles lord it over them, and their high officials exercise authority over them. Not so with you. Instead, whoever wants to become great among you must be your servant, and whoever wants to be first must be your slave—just as the Son of Man did not come to be served, but to serve, and to give his life as a ransom for many" (Matt. 20:25–28).

9. "If the relationship is abusive, either emotionally or physically, the wife *cannot* be asked to submit.... She should be advised to remove herself from danger. Truth and justice cannot be ignored. If a husband asks his wife to do something inappropriate for a Christian, again, she should not submit."[10] What are ways a Christian woman or child could handle such a situation?

10. Paul says slaves should work "as slaves of Christ, doing the will of God from your heart" (6:6). He also says that masters need to remember that they and their workers have the same Master, who values the worker as much as the boss (6:9). What would mutual submission look like for masters/employers? For slaves/workers?

11. Is it possible to live in mutual submission and still lead with confidence? Explain.

12. What do you think God wants you to do—or do differently—in, to, or for the Lord in your family or workplace?

RESPONDING TO GOD'S WORD

IN YOUR GROUP:

This is a good opportunity to pray for husbands, wives, parents, supervisors, and workers in the group. Ask each person, "How can we pray for you in your role as _____?" (Ask people to keep their answers brief, or it will take all night.) Then pray for that person briefly. This passage provides many specifics you can pray for different people. For instance, "Lord, give X the grace to love his wife as you love your church. Show him how he can help her grow in holiness...."

ON YOUR OWN:

Set either your job or your marriage before the Lord. Ask him to fill you with his Spirit (5:18) for insight about how to fulfill your role in him, to him, and for him.

IF FOCUSING ON YOUR MARRIAGE ...

You might exchange and talk with your spouse about a list of those things each would like the other to do to fulfill Paul's instructions to husbands and wives. Then pray as a couple or individually that how you relate to one another in mutual submission would always bring glory to the gospel of Jesus Christ.

IF FOCUSING ON YOUR JOB ...

Write down a list of questions you have for the Lord about your job. Write down any concerns. Write down at least five things you are thankful for, even something as basic as "I'm thankful that I have this job to pay my bills." Then spend a minute or two in silence, asking the Lord to show you how to live mutual submission in all relationships, regardless of whether you are in the role of a leader or a follower.

NOTES

1. This section is based on *NIVAC: Ephesians*, 158–159, 179, 184–186, 195–196.
2. This section is based on *NIVAC: Ephesians*, 285–333.
3. Snodgrass, 311.
4. Snodgrass, 292.
5. Snodgrass, 311.
6. Ibid.
7. Snodgrass, 312–313.
8. This section is based on *NIVAC: Ephesians*, 293–299, 319–333.
9. Snodgrass, 315.
10. Snodgrass, 316.

GOD'S STRENGTH
IN US

Ephesians 1:15 – 23; 3:1 – 21; 6:10 – 24

What do the films *Spider-Man* and *Pride and Prejudice* have in common? Both are about ordinary people graced with the power to do extraordinary things. In *Spider-Man*, superpowers enable nerdy Peter Parker to combat terrifying evildoers. In *Pride and Prejudice,* wit, courage, beautiful eyes, and circumstances enable Elizabeth Bennett to do something women everywhere long to do: transform a rich, handsome, and emotionally unavailable man into a man who can love her.

Most of us wish we had power to do things we seem helpless to affect. If only we could do something about Washington politics, about terrorists, about the way our employers run the company, about our wayward child, about the person whose love we long for. Some of us fear the forces of evil. Others have mundane but agonizing concerns.

"[S]tatistically Ephesians focuses on words for power more than any other New Testament letter."[1] Paul thinks it's vital for Christians to know the power that is ours for the asking.

HIS POWER FOR US[2]

Read Ephesians 1:15 – 23.

Paul prays for his readers to know several crucial things, one of which is God's "incomparably great power for us who believe" (1:19). How great is that power? Strong enough to raise a dead man and exalt him above all the spiritual and material powers.

GOING DEEPER

[The five categories of powers in Ephesians 1:21–22 refer to spiritual beings, but] no certain conclusions can be drawn about distinctions between these terms, and no hierarchy of the powers is in mind.[3]

1. Explain why it is important for us to know that "Whatever powers exist— real or imaginary, human or nonhuman—they are *all* subject to Christ."[4]

2. Paul's prayer points to God's power to bring life from death. Why do we need to be confident that this power is at work here and now?

Why do we need to be confident that God will raise us from the dead when Christ returns?

For many of us, "our image of God—the idol in our minds—does not merit contemplation, devotion, or obedience. Our God is too remote, disinterested, and inept. In fact, he is too much like us."[5] We desperately need to contemplate how mighty, loving, and active God really is.

THE POWER TO KNOW LOVE[6]

Read Ephesians 3:1–21.

Paul is in prison for the sake of Gentiles (non-Jews), including those to whom he's writing. For the second time in this letter he prays for them, and this time strength and power are major themes in his prayer.

3. Make a list of everything Paul says about strength or power in 3:14–21.

Strength from where? Strength to do what?

4. Why is it so important for us to know the vastness of Christ's love for us?

Many of us long for God to do something powerful in our circumstances or in other people—our boss or our loved one. Paul's original readers probably have family members and employers who oppose their faith, yet Paul doesn't pray here for God's power to change other people. He prays for God's power to be at work "in *your* inner being" (3:16), "in *your* hearts through faith" (3:17) and "within *us*" (3:20) [italics added].

5. Why do you suppose Paul focuses on praying for what happens inside us rather than around us?

All of Paul's teaching about how to live is within our ability because of God's power at work within us through his Spirit. He says: live worthy of your calling; imitate Christ; respond to what he's done; do everything as if you were doing it to the Lord and for the Lord. Paul prays for us to have power not to change our circumstances or other people, but to change *us*. The Spirit gives us the power to change how *we* deal with people and circumstances.

6. Are you more interested in power to change things around you, or to change you? Talk about why.

7. Paul prays for you not just to know *about* Christ's love, but to know his love. To know it by experience. You talked in session 4 about what helps or hinders you from knowing that love. Where are you now on that?

If we know intimately Christ's presence and love, the ethical teaching of Ephesians 4–6, and indeed all of the Christian life, falls into place. Knowing Christ's love—and having the Holy Spirit influence us at the core of our being—comes as a gift, but it doesn't happen by magic while we wait passively. "The Spirit will not empower unwilling, inattentive spirits."[7] He doesn't reveal Christ's love to hearts preoccupied with worldly things. We need to be aware of our need for him, attentive to his purposes and leading, giving time to our inner lives, and ready to be obedient.

THE POWER TO STAND FIRM[8] *Start*

Read Ephesians 6:10–20.

In his final instructions, Paul returns again to this theme of strength and power. He has talked about putting on our new self, who is like God in holiness and righteousness (4:24). Now he says we need to put on God's armor to stand against "the devil's schemes" (6:11).

8. What are some of "the devil's schemes" that Paul might be talking about here?

9. Christ has already triumphed over the spiritual forces of evil (1:20–22). Why then does Paul tell us here that we're engaged in a struggle in which we have to stand firm against them?

The pieces of armor (truth, righteousness, etc.) are not cute pictures, but realities about God and what he gives us that need to become realities about us and how we live. God gives us his own righteousness; we need to reflect that righteous character in our actions. He gives us faith and salvation; we need to live full of faith and confident of our salvation.

10. The armor strengthens you to stand against evil schemes and do what God wants done. Which aspect of the armor is hardest for you to wear consistently? What would wearing it involve for you?

11. The New Testament gives us little information about evil spiritual powers other than to say that they exist and that Christ has defeated them. From what Paul says in Ephesians, how much energy do you think we should devote to thinking about and combating evil spiritual powers?[9] Explain your view.

12. What insights will you take away from this study of Ephesians?

What action do you believe God is inviting you to take?

RESPONDING TO GOD'S WORD

IN YOUR GROUP:

Paul's prayers in 1:18–23 and 3:16–21 are both worth praying aloud together. Alternatively, you can pray in your own words based on Paul's prayers or use this prayer based on 3:16–21:

> *God our Father,*
> *We acknowledge that we and every other person has his or her origin in you.*
> *We owe you our lives.*
> *Forgive us for the arrogance of thinking we are better or more important than other people.*
> *Let your Spirit work in us to strengthen us. We want your Spirit to merge with ours.*
> *Make the presence of Christ so real that we sense your love and live from your love.*
> *Help us understand how deep your love is so that it changes us into your very image.*
> *You who are all powerful beyond anything we can conceive, we praise you. Every accolade of worth we throw at your feet. You alone are God. From your worth all other worth is determined.*
> *For the gift of life in Christ we and all your people worship you. Together and forever we will sing your praise. Amen.*[10]

ON YOUR OWN:

Write your own prayer based on 1:18–23 and 3:16–21. What do you need the power of God's Spirit to do?

NOTES

1. Snodgrass, 74.
2. This section is based on *NIVAC: Ephesians*, 70–92.
3. Snodgrass, 76.
4. Snodgrass, 77.
5. Snodgrass, 190.
6. This section is based on *NIVAC: Ephesians*, 157–192.
7. Snodgrass, 186.
8. This section is based on *NIVAC: Ephesians*, 334–361.
9. See Snodgrass, 347–354, for a discussion of demonic powers.
10. Snodgrass, 192.

Leader's Notes

1. We are the faithful. We are blessed in the heavenly realms with every spiritual blessing. We are those whom God chose to make holy and blameless, whom he chose to be for the praise of his glory. We have redemption and forgiveness. God "purposed in him" to bring unity to everything under Christ. We hope in him.

   "God's purpose and election take place in Christ (1:4, 9, 11). God's grace and redemption are found in Christ (1:6–7). All things in heaven and on earth are summed up in Christ (1:10). People hope in Christ, hear the word in Christ, and by faith are sealed in Christ (1:12–13). Remember that this whole section is worship: God is being praised, and the focus of that praise is what God has done in Christ and what is available in Christ."[1]

2. We become "included in Christ" by hearing and believing the gospel. This may be a good time to invite any in your group who are unsure if they are in Christ to pray, confessing that they are a sinner and affirming that Christ has died for their sins.

3. Talk about how your appearance, your clothing choices, your speech, your leisure activities, your work, your education, your food, your habits, your use of media, your use of money and time, and what you think is and isn't important in life are influenced by where you're from.

4. Most of us feel to some degree a tension between the values of the place where we live physically and those of the realm "in Christ."

5. Paul isn't saying we're sinless in this life. But he is saying that we're supposed to be increasingly set apart (that's what *holy* means) from the destructive habits of those who don't know God. Being in Christ is meant to transform our character, habits, ethics — the way we live all week long.

6. The ways of the world without God, the agenda of the Evil One, and our cravings (for possessions, sexual partners, stimulating experiences, admiration, and so on) used to determine who we were and how we lived. Apart from God, we are enslaved to the compulsions and emptiness of a self-focused life.

7. "'[H]eavenly realms' does not refer to a physical location but to a spiritual reality — God's world, in which believers have a share and which evil forces still seek to attack.... It is a way of saying that this world is not the only reality."[2] In the heavenly realms we have privilege, honor, security, responsibility. Christians today often speak of inviting Christ into their hearts, but Paul rarely speaks about having Christ in us, and often about having us in Christ. Likewise, he talks less often about our going to heaven when we die than he does about our living in the heavenly realms now.

8. Modern culture strokes our individualism. Advertising encourages us to customize everything for our individual taste. But Paul says we need to stop thinking of ourselves merely as individuals. We are part of Christ and of each other. We are "one new being," a single "body," a "building." It's not just that we're all going to heaven together — we are joined to each other in Christ *here and now*. This connected reality "is the root of the love, care, and justice Christians are to show."[3]

9. "The attitude of this world is best expressed in the phrase, 'You're different from me, and I resent you for that.' We *create* barriers between races, nations, religions, genders, social and economic classes, denominations, schools, communities, teams, and families.... [But to] maintain divisions is to deny what Christ has accomplished....

    "Nowhere is this theology more important for modern Christians than in dealing with *racial hostility*. Christians of other races are part of us, and divisions cannot be allowed to continue.... The point is not merely that all Christians are *equal*; rather, the point is that all Christians have been *joined*, which has far more significance and impact.

"If the barriers are down and we are joined to other believers, then several responses are required from Christians. (1) Acceptance and *valuing* people of other races on an equal level is a necessity. ...

"(2) In addition, we will need *investment* in Christians of other races. We cannot accept and value what we do not know or care about. We need to demonstrate that other groups matter to us. ...

"(3) We need to seek *justice* for other groups as well. Questions about justice are often complicated—witness the debate over illegal immigrants—but the church should be leading the discussion about justice and compassion so that whole groups of people are not placed on a second tier."[4]

10. "Differentiation is necessary for identity, but the human tendency to create *barriers* is a distortion and a sin. Distinction and uniqueness do not have to lead to division. The erection of barriers results from the ways we attribute value, that is, by devaluing those who are different."[5]

11. A sense that we belong enables us to relate and accomplish things. Families are supposed to be primary in giving us a sense of belonging, but often they don't, and then we find it hard to feel we belong somewhere as adults.

"This text says we *do* belong. Christ brought us home to God. We live in God's house as members of his family, and at the same time we are a house in which God lives (2:19–22). We belong with God and are involved in what he is doing. The other people in the house are family with us. This home defines us. ... A sense of family should shape our worship. Worship should not be like a production we watch; rather, we need the comfort and freedom of being involved in a family experience, joining together to communicate with God, to address and be addressed."[6]

NOTES

1. Snodgrass, 47.
2. Ibid.
3. Snodgrass, 147.
4. Snodgrass, 150–151.
5. Snodgrass, 150.
6. Snodgrass, 149.

SESSION 2 LEADER'S NOTES

1. There are many good, ethical people who don't seem to fit Paul's description. "Paul is not denying the value of creation or of humanity created in the image of God. He is not saying all human beings are worthless, nor is his primary concern what will happen on Judgment Day. His concern is to contrast the plight of humanity without God with the privilege of humanity with God and in Christ....

   "[W]e need only to reflect on the evil in our own society, our suicide rate, the enormous problems caused by escapism through alcohol and drugs, and the meaninglessness that challenges all of us as we face injustice, disease, and our own death. Death haunts us and is our destiny. If we also remember that fully one billion people live in dire poverty and that war and terrorism afflict the planet, 'living death' may be too soft a description."[1]

2. Paul's description is so bleak that "it would be easy to reject the world and all association with unbelievers. But a healthy theology of creation does not allow rejection of humanity or the material world and enjoyment of it. God announced his creation good (Gen. 1), and this assumption is fundamental to Paul's theology (see 1 Cor. 10:26; 1 Tim. 4:4). 'Separation from the world' is not to be taken lightly, but that teaching does not mean disrespect for or distancing ourselves from unbelievers (1 Cor. 5:9 – 10). The attitude that God's people take toward unbelievers must mirror the love described in Ephesians 2:4 – 10."[2]

3. Paul highlights:

   - God's great love for us
   - Salvation — rescue from destruction; grace — God's "completely undeserved, loving commitment ... to us"[3]
   - Living simultaneously in this world and in the heavenly realms
   - A future that involves ages of experiencing God's grace
   - The opportunity to do good works that God has prepared for us

4. We might "take God's love for granted with no impact on our lives or we [might] reject that God could love someone as sinful and/or insignificant as we are."[4]

5. Some group members may have experience feeling like outsiders. Others who have grown up in the church or have always been "good" people may find it harder to relate to that outsider status. This question and question #6 are opportunities for group members to learn about each other. Our past experiences have great influence on how we respond to statements in Scripture, and it's helpful to see that through our own and each other's stories.

6. This is a chance to hear and encourage group members for whom walls have been a way of life. You can help group members be honest if you, as leader, are willing to be honest about areas in which you have trouble fully living what Paul describes. If you send the message that it's easy for you to have no walls between you and God or others, and if that's not entirely true, then ironically you are erecting a wall between you and the group.

7. Remembering who we used to be fosters gratitude for what God has done for us. Remembering who we are now helps us resist slipping back into the habits of our old life.

   "For some people past memories are so painful that they cannot be forgotten, and no suggestion is made that such memories can be easily erased. But Christians must know that the only event that defines us is Christ's death and resurrection, in which we are involved. We die to self—both the sinful self and the self sinned against—and rise to new life in Christ.... The old reality still must be faced, but newness in Christ is the defining force.

   "A woman who has been raped cannot forget the violation against her, but must the violation continue as an open wound or scar preventing life? Or can life defined by Christ bring healing and wholeness?... We cannot always choose what happens to us, but we can choose—at least to some degree—what power it will be granted."[5]

8. Film and TV are full of examples of meaninglessness, darkness, insensitivity, and refusal to know the truth. So are many families, schools, and workplaces, as well as many events in the economic and political arenas.

9. Sensual people often think they feel things deeply, that they pursue sensual pleasures because they enjoy life. They may be unaware of the numbness at their core that leads them to seek stimulation through more and more extreme experiences.

10. Christ-centered thinking makes the heart sensitive to God's desires and others' needs. It refuses to be deadened to pain even when life is painful. It refuses denial, but faces the truth even when the truth is difficult. It therefore opens the mind to the light and joy and hope of a truth that can be relied on. It draws life and strength from God. It thereby sees through confusion to wise decisions. It finds meaning in opportunities to love and serve. It knows that this life isn't all there is, so it frees a person from a life that is a futile exercise ending in death.

11. A Christ-centered person can enjoy physical pleasures as the fruits of God's good creation. He or she enjoys them in moderation—reasonable amounts, in appropriate contexts that build rather than destroy life. The more alive a person is, the more he or she can enjoy small and simple pleasures without craving more and more and more. "Desires are not bad in themselves. They are God-given assistants for living, but they need a Lord. Give them one."[6]

12. This view of conversion requires more from us than mere intellectual assent to some statements about Jesus. That can be uncomfortable if we don't like to think in communion with God, if we don't enjoy reflecting on what's going on inside us and why we do what we do. If we like operating on autopilot, this constant putting off the old and putting on the new will challenge us.

    "Salvation is totally the work of God in which we are totally involved. This alone does justice to the thought of being in Christ. . . .

    "Biblical texts can be produced to suggest that change occurs at baptism, repeatedly throughout life, or at the end of time.[7] Once again the now and not-yet character of Christian faith is obvious. A change has already occurred, is occurring, and will be completed at the end of time. What happened at baptism is a real putting off of self and a putting on of Christ. If there is no transformation, there is no salvation. But this is *not* merely a decision or a one-time event. *Conversion is a process*, as the present tense of 4:23 shows convincingly."[8]

NOTES

1. Snodgrass, 108–109.
2. Snodgrass, 108.

3. Snodgrass, 103.
4. Snodgrass, 112.
5. Snodgrass, 147–148.
6. Snodgrass, 244.
7. For instance, at baptism, Galatians 3:27; repeatedly, Romans 13:12–14; at the end of time, 1 Corinthians 15:53–54; 2 Corinthians 5:2–4.
8. Snodgrass, 241.

SESSION 3 LEADER'S NOTES

1. Understanding that Christians are saved by God's grace alone is the key to overcoming both ego and shame. It gives us the gratitude we need to love God passionately and actively. "Virtually all our experience tells us that we have to earn acceptance, love, and respect. We spend our lives seeking self-actualization, some act or fact that will give us significance and standing. If we have self-confidence, we see no need to be stripped of all our hard-earned value. Other people are worse than we are, so why shouldn't God accept us? If we lack self-confidence, we find it hard to think God will accept us under any circumstance. Either way, grace is so hard to take.... [By contrast] Grace moves us to worship and true humility."[1]

2. We can mentally accept ideas without acting on them. But truly relying on someone means taking action on that trust. It's the act of stepping out on a bridge, trusting that it will support our weight. To refuse to take the step, and the next step, and the next, is to prove that we don't really trust the one we claim to be relying on. "To say 'I have faith' does not so much say anything about oneself; rather it says, 'God is a trustworthy God.'"[2]

3. God created us. He chose us before he made the world. He adopted us as his heirs. He sent Christ to rescue us from slavery to sin. He endured suffering for our sake. He has been consistently faithful to his promises. He is reliable. The resurrection of Christ proves that God is able to do exactly what he says he will.

4. Being saved *by* works would mean that our deeds win us status or privilege before God. But nothing we can do can put a claim on God. We have nothing to boast about.

   Being saved *for* works means that our actions still matter. Our works don't put a claim on God, but they do God's work in the world. They fulfill what we were made for. As a response of gratitude, not a gesture of pride or guilt or fear, they have value. "God planned and acted not only to save, but also to mark out the way we should live. John Stott's words are not too strong: 'Good works are indispensable to salvation—not as its ground or means ... but as its consequence and evidence.'"[3]

5. This notion is a reaction against the idea that salvation is a transaction with God to get us into heaven. The Reformers like Martin Luther were

right to oppose schemes that promised to earn (or buy) one's way into heaven. But the Reformers never imagined that Christians might swing to the opposite extreme and think that, once they got confirmed plane tickets to heaven, they could sin as much as they liked. The New Testament consistently says we're here on earth for more than that. "[W]e distort the very idea of faith when we fail to see that it joins us to Christ and affects the whole reality of our lives. The faith that many people profess is nothing more than a false and *groundless* hope of escaping judgment. We do nothing to gain our salvation and life with God, *but such a joining to God does everything to us.*"4 If it doesn't, it's a delusion.

6. "Unfortunately, Christians have as hard a time with pride as anyone."5 We don't have to work to make God happy or to prove ourselves better than others, especially non-Christians. The only works worth doing are acts of love fueled by grace and gratitude. When he spoke of " 'good works' Paul was not thinking about 'do-goodism,' but about a life reflective of God's love."6

7. Habits of a child of light express goodness, righteousness (living according to God's character), and truth. Children of light seek to discern what will please the Lord (out of love, not guilt or fear). They avoid addictive behaviors like drunkenness and sexual promiscuity that give a false sense of aliveness to numbed souls. They do what is right even when no one is looking—as if everything we do is open to the light for all to see.

8. Darkness symbolizes deceit and hiding. People who do wrong prefer to hide it so that no one can see. So darkness can symbolize acts of evil in general. Light represents goodness, integrity, truthfulness, and a lack of deceit and hiding.

9. Telling people what they want to hear instead of what is true isn't love. It's deceit. Love doesn't mean bashing people with harsh "truth," and it doesn't require that we tell everything to everybody. Love requires discernment about when to speak. But love doesn't wear a mask to make oneself look better than one is. Love doesn't avoid uncomfortable truths that require something of us. Love sometimes confronts others, but it does so wisely, with patience.

10. Harshness tells people they don't deserve value and respect, and that's a lie. Arrogance tells people we matter more than they do, and that too is a lie.

It's essential that we get our own egos out of the way before we approach someone to deal with their faults.

11. We fear rejection and ridicule—and often with good reason. We've created a church culture that teaches people that the goal is to look perfect. That culture is harmful because it hinders people from facing and getting help for their sin. It also hinders people from experiencing the comfort amid pain that they're supposed to get from God's people. We need to dismantle that idea about looking perfect and build a church culture that teaches that the goal is to have integrity, to be honest and vulnerable with each other, to be trustworthy when others tell the truth about themselves, and to help each other grow toward maturity.

12. Some of us have too much self-doubt, and some of us have too little. Those with too much self-doubt have trouble seeing the ways in which God is doing his work through them. They need to relax and focus on God's love for them. They need to trust his grace. On the other hand, those of us with too little self-doubt may think we have faith when we don't, and that can have serious eternal consequences. Also, those with little self-doubt may be arrogant with no sense of their need. Those among us who are highly self-confident and thick-skinned may need to hear firmer words from God than the more tenderhearted among us need.

NOTES

1. Snodgrass, 120–121.
2. Snodgrass, 105.
3. Snodgrass, 107.
4. Snodgrass, 114.
5. Snodgrass, 121.
6. Ibid.

SESSION 4 LEADER'S NOTES

1. We are called to be "in Christ." To be holy and blameless (1:4)—that is, to be set apart from selfish agendas and full of integrity. Christians are called to be his heirs, his beloved children (1:5). To be in unity with him, and especially with the rest of his body (1:10; 2:16–22). To cause his glorious nature to be praised (1:12). To be in Christ means to be sealed with the Holy Spirit (1:13). To be alive and seated with Christ in the heavenly realms (2:5–6). To do good works he has prepared for us (2:10). To be fellow citizens with God's people and members of God's household, and together with them to be a holy temple where God dwells (2:19–22). Together—not on our own—we are called to be his body, his temple.

2. Rules don't motivate truly ethical behavior. One can obey some rules out of guilt, fear of exposure, or fear of punishment. But nobody loves, forgives, or is compassionate out of guilt or fear. Awareness of God, of being loved, is the only reliable motive for biblical ethics.

3. Self-centeredness is unworthy of people who are called by a God who gives of himself. It's unworthy of people who are called to be united in one body with others. Humility isn't weakness or doubting our abilities. It's about valuing others and God. "It is an awareness that all we are and have is from God. The humble person refuses to value self above others or to assign more privilege or importance to self than to others.... Egotism, on the other hand, is an idolatry of the self, the failure to realize that God is the pattern for life, not us."[1]

4. Grace is opposed to earning one's salvation; it is not opposed to the effort required to live in a way that pleases God. Many of us have been trained in spiritual laziness—we expect to work hard to achieve success in our careers, but it comes as a shock that anything is required of us in our spiritual lives. Some of us may have to direct less energy into achieving by the world's standards so we have more energy to devote to cultivating Christlike character. The effort doesn't go into church activity (as important as that may be) but to prayer and attention to how we treat people.

5. Unity involves peace rather than fighting with other believers. It involves sensing our connectedness, our need for each other, like the parts of a

body. It doesn't mean agreeing about everything or doing things the same way; in fact, unity involves a diversity of gifts. But it does mean all Christians focus on one Lord and one hope. It involves Christian leaders equipping people to build up the body, with everybody aiming toward unity and mature Christlike character. Unity protects us from deceitful teachers. Speaking and doing the truth in love is a key feature of unity.

"How can unity be established? It does not need to be established, for it already exists, given by God. It needs to be valued and maintained.... Our concern is not for some organizational unity. Rather, the concern is unity *in Christ*, which carries with it an assumption of the biblical message about Christ as crucified and risen Lord. Christians do not need to agree on everything to have unity; we need to live the unity of a common commitment to Christ. The formula of Rupert Meldenius popularized by Richard Baxter is still good guidance: 'Unity in essentials, liberty in incidentals, and in all things charity [love].'"[2]

6–7. Responding to what God has done for us: We are all members of one body. Don't grieve the Holy Spirit or give the devil a foothold. Share with those in need. Speak to benefit others. (These last two are reflections of God as much as they are responses.)

Reflecting God's character: Avoid bitterness as God does. Be kind and forgiving as God is. Walk in love as Christ loved.

8. You may need to give people time to talk about this. Sometimes past hurts hinder us from believing God loves us. People need to experience Christian love now—in places like your small group.

9. Our highly individualistic society ingrains perceptions that we have to unlearn in order see ourselves as connected. Think about the messages of self-reliance and self-importance you get from advertising, from TV and movie heroes, from your families. "It's up to you." "Have it your way." "Customize it the way you want." "Be whoever you want to be."

10. Time alone in a quiet place with the TV and phone turned off is a big help in overcoming such habits. Spend that time reflecting on how God is the center of the universe—and you aren't. Reflect on his love for you and how he has provided for your needs. Reflect on his forgiveness and patience toward you. Find one friend you can trust and ask for help and prayer in overcoming your anger. Just admitting you don't have total

control is a big step. Take responsibility when you're angry; don't blame the other person for making you angry. Look for opportunities to be helpful, especially in your family. Practice saying, "I'm sorry." If you're angry at someone who is doing something wrong, ask your trusted friend to help you strategize ways of dealing with that person that will solve the problem and that don't involve steaming in silence or blowing up.

11. We need to be gentle, patient, forgiving, and loving to such people. We also need to protect ourselves and others from their hostility. Boundaries can be loving, not vengeful. We need to help spouses and children remove themselves (temporarily or permanently) from situations where a family member yells, makes cruel comments, or is violent. Those who don't live with such people can often just respond to an angry person with kindness and firmness. Those who do live with them may need support to say, "If you're going to yell, I'm going to leave the room."

12. It's essential that everyone see the difference between legalism and responding in gratitude to what God has done for us.

NOTES

1. Snodgrass, 209–210.
2. Snodgrass, 210–211.

SESSION 5 LEADER'S NOTES

1. Our society is anti-hierarchy. We like networks of peers. Paul presents the body of Christ as a network of peers headed by somebody who is not a peer. It may be helpful for group members to voice reasons why they have trouble trusting an authority figure, even God—maybe especially God. People who have been hurt by authority figures need to be heard and understood.[1]

2. We will value their wants and needs at least as much as our own. That doesn't mean ceasing to value our own needs. It means giving up self-centeredness.

3. We might listen to others more, let them have their way more, treat them with more respect. For example, "Mutual submission should be applied to current discussions of worship styles. To insist that worship can take place in only one manner is myopic and limits the expression of the whole body. Mutual submission requires the humility to listen, tolerate, be taught, and be enriched by the worship of others, so long as it is within legitimate bounds.

   "A further place where mutual submission has application concerns money. Usually we allow our society to dictate how money is used, assigned, and hoarded. Mutual submission is disturbing to this society's dictates, for it requires reconsideration of how wages are determined and how wealth is shared."[2]

4. "Mutual submission will not allow us to promote ourselves and our own interests, but neither does it make us 'doormats' to be used by others. *Legitimate* submission cannot be coerced. The text assumes that everyone in the community is supported and enhanced. Where that does not take place, a person will have to be wise enough to discern whether to forego his or her own rights or seek justice. Christ's pattern of self-giving love does not mean that we can never seek justice for ourselves. Jesus did not acquiesce to Herod or the Pharisees, and Paul did not hesitate to defend himself or speak strongly to the Galatians or Corinthians. Submission will mean that even in seeking justice, we are motivated by love for others in the community, rather than by love of self."[3]

5. We'll remember that we and the other person are peers, but Christ is our Master and is watching whether we seek to exalt ourselves above others. We don't submit to others because we're afraid of them. Because of Christ, we have no reason to fear them. We submit to people because we know we're not the center of the universe.

6. Such a man as described in this question would expect Paul to focus only on supporting the man's authority. Perhaps the most astonishing part of Paul's instruction to husbands and masters is that it is a specific instance of the broader instruction, "Submit to one another out of reverence for Christ" (5:21). Mutual submission doesn't come easily to men accustomed to power, but Paul expects husbands and masters to voluntarily set their self-interest aside for the benefit of their wives and workers. Husbands and masters are to value their wives and workers as much as they value themselves. Wives and workers aren't subordinates whom they can control and treat however they like. Demeaning or exploiting a wife or worker, much less harming them, is biblically unacceptable.

7. Paul defines headship as the man's responsibility to give of himself for the care of his wife. Headship means being responsible. Instead of telling the wife to nurture her husband, Paul tells the husband to nurture his wife. Instead of treating her like she's ignorant, the husband is supposed to make sure she gets whatever she needs for her spiritual growth. Ironically, the husband's leadership is for the wife's benefit. Husbands are to be motivated by what Christ has done for them because Christ is their Master.

8. Human authorities aren't lord over us in the way Christ is Lord over us. But we give them respect and honor because of our respect and honor for Christ. Our relation to the Lord is the motivation for our relation to other authorities. But, of course, if human authorities ask us to do something that would dishonor Christ, our submission to him comes first, regardless of human displeasure. Christ is head over all. And submission doesn't mean keeping our mouths shut and following orders. It means fully engaging all our gifts, including our ideas. Mutual submission means giving up self-centeredness and promoting the good of our husbands or wives, parents or children, employers or employees—indeed everyone with whom we are in relationship.

9. Submission to the Lord obliges a wife or child to say no when a husband or parent sins to the extent of abusiveness or immorality. Allowing a husband to do evil is not serving him. The church needs to stand vigorously against domestic violence and exploitation and support family members in stopping such sins. A husband's headship never authorizes him to harm or exploit his wife or children, and wives may need to separate temporarily or permanently from husbands who so grossly misunderstand the responsibility the Lord has given them.

10. Some possibilities for all, since most managers are also workers: Working diligently, not cutting corners, respecting all coworkers, not stealing company supplies. But also saying no to unethical business practices or the exploitation of workers, because of reverence for the Lord as the higher Master.

11. There is no greater confidence than knowing we are living rightly before God who knows the hearts of all involved. Leading with integrity and respect for others will more likely get a better response than leading by putting ourselves first and lording over others.

12. As leader, it will be helpful for you to think of something specific the Lord is putting on your heart. How can you do unto others not just the way you want them to do unto you, but as if they were Christ, as if you were Christ, and because of Christ?

NOTES

1. Snodgrass, 184–186, addresses the concerns some people have about calling God "Father."
2. Snodgrass, 312.
3. Snodgrass, 311–312.

SESSION 6 LEADER'S NOTES

1. "Because no other power can rival [Christ], and because in him the fullness of God lives, Christians do not have to look elsewhere to find what they need for life. What they need is in Christ. This power, however, is not power in the abstract; it is *relational power*— power that is known because of being bound to the one in whom power resides.

   "But looking elsewhere is precisely what many people do. A strange temptation prevails to mix faith in Christ with some other ingredient.... But Christ is sufficient and nothing else is needed. *To attempt to add to Christ is to take away from him....* [We can] focus on Christ, rejoice, and live confidently.... Evil is real, and as far as we can tell, so are spiritual beings, but they are not mentioned in this passage because they are a threat or should be a cause of concern. Instead, they are defeated and we need not worry."[1]

   Some group members interested in spiritual warfare may take a different view of spiritual powers, and you can have a lively discussion. See *The NIV Application Commentary: Ephesians* for more on this topic.

2. "The brevity, injustice, suffering, and dying in this life cry out for the ultimate victory of God, for God to do something.... God has done something marvelous and is not finished.... For those attempting to focus only on pleasure in this life, Christianity has the responsibility of removing society's insulation from the truth of the hardship of life and of death. Without being morbid and without neglecting the legitimacy of pleasure and life, we must face and embrace both suffering and death. The gospel allows us to do just that.

   "For those who know this life is temporary and feel its meaninglessness, we convey the hope of God's future, when he has a people for himself. Even those looking into death's face can have hope. Without diminishing the awful pain of diseases like AIDS and cancer, people can know God is bigger than disease, that he does not leave them, and that he holds out his future to them."[2]

3. The strength we need comes through the Spirit working in our inner being. Active faith in Christ opens us to that power. God's power is already at work in us. His power is huge; he can do far more than we can ask

or imagine. The main power we need is to experience and comprehend Christ's love.

4. God's love fuels us for everything else. He gives his power primarily so that we can love him and other people, even in difficult circumstances. And the main thing that enables us to love difficult people is knowing that we're deeply and completely loved by God. We don't have to spend our energy trying to get people to validate and appreciate us if we have that from Christ.

5. It's essential that we grasp God's agenda. He's not primarily interested in making our lives pleasant. He's interested in freeing us from self-centeredness and making us people who love others deeply and wisely. Learning to love is what this life is about, and love is what we'll spend eternity doing.

6. As leader, it may be helpful for you to come clean on this. If we're honest, most of us will admit we're not as eager to learn to love as God would like us to be.

7. This is so important that it's worth reviewing, but don't let the talkative people dominate. If they had their say in session 4, you might invite others to talk.

8. In the context of what Paul has been talking about throughout this letter, he's probably thinking of the devil's schemes to keep us from loving one another, from living as the unified members of one body that we truly are, from believing we're loved and living as loved people. He's probably not talking about demonic attacks on the church from unbelievers. He's probably talking about apathy and the lack of love within us and among us.

9. They are defeated but can still deceive us if we let them. "Evil is ... a rebellion against God and the boundaries and values he designated.... Evil entices us to change the boundaries so that God does not receive the allegiance we owe and so that property, life, and the dignity of others is redefined in our favor. Evil has its roots at the center of our being in our attempt to obtain the best for ourselves. This is why evil is a trap; it always looks like something good for us, but it does not ask about God or other people, and it does not ask about long term effects....

   "The spiritual forces of evil in Ephesians are trap setters, seeking to delude us into shifting the boundaries.... In most cases our choice is not between obvious evil and something good but between two seemingly good and right options.... Evil traps us with the good, only slightly out of bounds. Each choice slightly out of bounds redraws the boundaries until nothing remains of God's intent."[3]

11. "[T]he goal is to avoid evil, not focus on it. Christians often make the error of giving the devil way more than *it* is due. The devil is more interesting to them than God, and *it* gets more attention....

"Focus on evil or the devil has several negative consequences, among which are: (1) Attention is diverted from God to evil. (2) Responsibility for evil is shifted from our own depravity to something outside us. (3) Confession and change are made more difficult. (4) Our sense of strength and courage is diminished.

"By focusing on evil we destroy ourselves; by focusing on God we find life and protection. God deserves our attention; evil does not. In asking us to put on the armor of God, the text directs our attention away from evil and to God and his purposes."[4]

NOTES

1. Snodgrass, 91.
2. Snodgrass, 90.
3. Snodgrass, 356–357.
4. Snodgrass, 357.

The NIV Application Commentary

Ephesians

Klyne Snodgrass

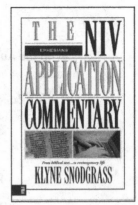

Most Bible commentaries take us on a one-way trip from the twentieth century to the first century. But they leave us there, assuming that we can somehow make the return journey on our own. In other words, they focus on the original meaning of the passage but don't discuss its contemporary application. The information they offer is valuable—but the job is only half done!

The NIV Application Commentary Series helps us with both halves of the interpretive task. This new and unique series shows readers how to bring an ancient message into a modern context. It explains not only what the Bible meant but also how it can speak powerfully today.

The great wisdom in the book of Ephesians, as Klyne Snodgrass so ably demonstrates, is its emphasis on both change and choice as the twin pillars of the gospel. One cannot exist without the other. And the place that change and choice ever and again come together is in our liturgy and worship. Ephesians is filled with prayer and praise for our great and sovereign Lord, who shows us, as we worship him, that one cannot become a new creature without acting like one, and that knowing how to act can only come if one recognizes the great change brought about in the new life in Jesus Christ.

Hardcover, Printed: 978-0-310-49340-2

Pick up a copy today at your favorite bookstore!

Share Your Thoughts

With the Author: Your comments will be forwarded to
the author when you send them to *zauthor@zondervan.com*.

With Zondervan: Submit your review of this book
by writing to *zreview@zondervan.com*.

Free Online Resources at
www.zondervan.com/hello

Zondervan AuthorTracker: Be notified whenever your
favorite authors publish new books, go on tour, or post
an update about what's happening in their lives.

Daily Bible Verses and Devotions: Enrich your life
with daily Bible verses or devotions that help you start
every morning focused on God.

Free Email Publications: Sign up for newsletters on
fiction, Christian living, church ministry, parenting, and
more.

Zondervan Bible Search: Find and compare
Bible passages in a variety of translations at
www.zondervanbiblesearch.com.

Other Benefits: Register yourself to receive online
benefits like coupons and special offers, or to participate
in research.